A Stoic's Guide to Personal Finance

Financial Security Through Discipline

Table of Contents

Chapter 1. Introduction

Immerse yourself into the captivating realm of personal finance guided by the enduring wisdom of Stoicism with our Special Report, "A Stoic's Guide to Personal Finance: Financial Security Through Discipline." Our enlightening journey is neither too technical nor too simplistic, striking a perfect balance for learners of all levels. Explore how the discipline and perspective of Stoicism can provide a unique, tranquil approach to managing your resources efficiently. Be prepared to uncover hidden practical insights to secure your financial future, rooted in ancient philosophy. This engaging and accessible guide is sure to empower you to take control of your financial destiny and lead a more fulfilled life. Order this illuminating special report now, reshape your finances, and persist on your pathway to financial stability with a pinch of Stoic serenity!

Chapter 2. Understanding Stoicism: An Introduction

Before we delve into understanding the nexus of Stoicism and personal finance, it is essential to decipher the profound philosophy of Stoicism itself. Widely adopted by the ancient Greeks and Romans, Stoicism is more than a philosophy; it's a way of life that encourages individuals to live their lives in harmony with nature and the universe.

2.1. The Birth of Stoicism

Stoicism was founded by Zeno of Citium in the early 3rd century BCE in Athens. Dissatisfied with the philosophies of his time, Zeno crafted a philosophy that emphasized inner tranquility, moral virtue, and self-control. His teachings attracted a large following and later influenced some of the greatest minds of ancient times, including Seneca, Epictetus, and Marcus Aurelius.

2.2. Key Principles of Stoicism

Stoicism is grounded in four primary virtues: wisdom (practical insights), temperance (moderation), justice (fairness), and courage (strength in face of adversity). Understanding these principles is the first step on the path to becoming Stoic.

1. **Wisdom:** It's the ability to distinguish what's within our control and what is not. Stoics believe your thoughts and actions are within your control, and everything else—be it external events or outcomes—is not.

2. **Temperance:** This implies the practice of discipline and self-control. The more we control our needs and desires, the less vulnerable we are to external circumstances.

3. **Justice:** Stoicism advocates treating others with fairness and kindness, which reflects on our actions and contributes to societal harmony.

4. **Courage:** This involves making right decisions despite fear and maintaining moral integrity even in the face of adversity.

2.3. Stoic Perspective on Emotion and Desire

Stoics often have an unfair reputation of being emotionless or devoid of desire. However, they were anything but. Stoics were keen on curbing negative emotions like anger, jealousy, or sadness resulting from attachment towards material objects or people. They encouraged detachment—not from feelings—but from hedonistic pleasures to attain true contentment.

However, they equally advocated for the fostering of positive emotions—those that lead to fortitude, humility, and empathy. Rather than suppressing desires, Stoics advise channeling them towards the betterment of self and society.

2.4. Stoic Practices

Stoicism isn't simply a trove of knowledge; it's a philosophy intended to be lived. Here are a few essential practices that, when incorporated into your life, can enhance your understanding of Stoic philosophy.

1. **Negative Visualization:** This practice involves visualizing worst-case scenarios. By frequently reflecting on the impermanence of things we hold dear, we learn to value them more and build resilience for when things go awry.

2. **The Dichotomy of Control:** Stoics constantly remind themselves of things they can control—mainly their actions and

judgments—and learn to be indifferent to what they can't. This practice is key to maintaining tranquility.

3. **Practicing Discomfort:** This could involve skipping a meal, taking a cold shower, or sleeping on the floor. The purpose isn't to inflict distress but to build resilience towards hardships.

2.5. Stoicism Today and Its Relevance

Stoicism continues to be influential, offering valuable lessons on confronting life's adversities. Business leaders, entrepreneurs, athletes, and everyday people have found solace and strength in its teachings. Stoicism provides a framework for managing stress, making decisions, interacting with others, and ultimately, experiencing a fulfilling life.

In the world of personal finance, Stoicism offers a unique perspective. By applying Stoic principles, one can achieve tranquility amid the financial turmoil, make wiser financial decisions, pursue wealth without greed, and manage losses with grace. Indeed, Stoicism can guide your journey towards financial security through a path of discipline, perspective, and tranquility.

By now, hopefully, you have a fundamental understanding of Stoicism: its origins, principles, practices, and relevance to today's world. Through the subsequent sections of this report, we will delve into how Stoicism can inform and enrich your personal financial journey, ensuring you gain not just wealth, but wisdom along the way.

Chapter 3. Personal Finance and Stoicism: The Connection

In the realm of personal finance, feelings often govern decisions. Whether it's the fear that comes with a dwindling bank account, or the excitement over stock market gains, our emotions can drive impulsive decisions that spiral us further away from our financial goals. But what if we could navigate the turbulent seas of finance with an even keel, drawing from an ancient philosophy? Stoicism, a school of thought dating back to the Hellenistic period, can provide an unexpected compass.

3.1. Stoicism: An Overview

Nurtured in Athens around the third century BCE, Stoicism held that peace and serenity stem from accepting the world as it is. Stoics strive to react not to external occurrences, but to their personal attitudes about those events. This indivisible thread between Stoicism and personal finance surfaces when our emotional reactions — such as panic at a market downturn — steer us off course. Just as Stoics cultivate indifference towards life's ebbs and flows, becoming financially stoic requires treating financial gains and losses with equanimity.

3.2. The Four Cardinal Virtues of Stoicism and Their Financial Implications

Central to the understanding of Stoicism are four cardinal virtues: Wisdom, Courage, Justice, and Temperance. Under the financial lens, these virtues translate into discerning decision-making, bravery in the face of financial uncertainties, fairness in monetary affairs, and measured spending.

1. **Wisdom**: In Stoicism, wisdom entails knowledge and the logical application of it. For personal finance, wisdom involves understanding financial concepts, such as investing, budgeting, and planning for retirement. The more knowledge you gather, the more equipped you are to make logical financial decisions, eliminating the emotional biases that can compromise your financial stability.

2. **Courage**: It takes courage to face financial realities and uncertainties. For Stoics, courage is not recklessness but the ability to confront situations with calm and resolution. In terms of personal finance, it could mean investing cautiously during market swings or making difficult decisions like job transitions or moving homes for a lower cost of living.

3. **Justice**: Justice, in Stoicism, implies fair dealings and harmony in relationships. In a financial context, this could mean paying fair wages to employees, honoring debts and obligations, and ensuring that your financial choices do not serve your interests at the expense of others'.

4. **Temperance**: The virtue of temperance is about moderation and self-control. In the world of finance, temperance informs controlled spending, curbing the penchant for impulsive purchases, and maintaining a balanced budget even in the face of attractive, but ultimately frivolous, products and services.

3.3. Stoicism: The Antidote to Lifestyle Inflation

One major financial problem we face is lifestyle inflation - increasing our expenditure as our income grows. Life upgrades, such as a bigger home or a fancier car, may bring transient joy, but they don't add to our financial stability. Through the lens of Stoicism, these acquisitions are external events that should not impact our happiness or financial decisions. By following the Stoic principles of differentiating between needs and wants, we can combat lifestyle inflation, accumulate wealth, and strengthen our financial security.

3.4. Stoicism and Investment

When it comes to investment decisions, emotions frequently lead the way, often causing hasty responses to market volatility. To detach emotions from investing, Stoicism offers the concept of the Dichotomy of Control: accepting we control our actions and responses, but not the results. As investors, we control our investment approach, risk tolerance, and the degree of diversification in our portfolio. Market performance, however, remains beyond our control. Understanding this distinction can bring about serenity in financial decision-making, fostering long-term investment strategies over short-term market reactions.

3.5. Conclusion: Towards a Stoic Approach to Personal Finance

Stoicism encourages indifference towards wealth and external riches with the knowledge that genuine happiness stems from within. This principle helps instill a balanced attitude towards money, acknowledging it as a tool for life rather than its ultimate goal.

By exploring and embracing the principles of Stoicism, we can navigate our financial future with a balanced insight and build a profound level of financial security, liberating ourselves from the fickle ebb and flow of ever-changing personal finance landscapes.

Consider these Stoic principles as a part of your financial strategy. They may result in not only an improved financial situation but also a more serene and more enjoyable life journey. After all, in the grand scope of life, finance is but a small (although important) part of our existence.

Thus, the profound wisdom of Stoicism can compellingly inform our approach to personal finance. By fostering discipline, understanding, and serenity, we can manage our finances more efficiently, mitigate emotional reactions, and ensure a secure financial future.

Chapter 4. Perception of Wealth: Shaping Your Financial Mindset

Modern society bombards us with images of excessive opulence, extravagant lifestyles, and ceaseless consumption, forming an elaborate illusion around the concept of wealth. To reshape this perception and anchor it in the ethos of Stoicism, we must first disassemble the myth, understanding wealth not as an absolute, desirable state but as a tool to facilitate life.

4.1. Discerning Wealth from Materialism

Wealth should not be confused with materialism. The former represents a state of having resources, while the latter is a pursuit for resources that often leads to an endless rat race. As Epictetus, a famous Stoic philosopher, said, "Wealth consists not in having great possessions, but in having few wants." The crux of this quote lies in understanding that desires for material goods form an insatiable appetite, leading to a cycle of perpetual want. On the other hand, wealth can serve as a buffer in life, shielding us against emergencies and facilitating our pursuit of a good life.

4.2. Redefining Wealth

Redefining wealth in our perspective involves acknowledging that it transcends mere currency and tangible assets. It envelops elements that add significant, lasting value to life, such as relationships, knowledge, experiences, health, and peace of mind. A stoic views wealth as a means to an end – a tool that enables the pursuit of virtue and tranquillity.

The Stoics ushered in a philosophy of indifference towards wealth, forewarning about the potential miseries attached to an insatiable desire for it. As Seneca once said, "To really, know what wealth is, have something of your own."

4.3. Cultivating a Stoic Approach to Wealth

The stoic emphasis is on self-discipline, mindfulness, and the pursuit of virtue. From this vantage point, financial prosperity is considered neutral—it is neither good nor bad. Recognizing that having control over our reactions to wealth is vital. You may not control the changing tides of the economy, your job security, or unexpected financial emergencies, but how you respond to them is within your purview.

The stoic practice of negative visualization can be aptly applied here. By routinely meditating on setbacks, like job loss, financial downtrends, and emergencies, we not only cultivate gratitude for current stability but also mentally equip ourselves to handle such situations if they materialize.

4.4. Wealth as a Tool, Not a Destination

The Stoics advise us to understand wealth as a tool and not a destination. Wealth can open doors, provide security, and offer opportunities. Conversely, the inappropriate use or intense pursuit of wealth can lead to a destructive cycle of endless craving, dissatisfaction, and anguish.

Epictetus stated: "Wealth consists not in having great possessions, but in having few wants." This implies that one needs to master the art of discernment, distinguishing between needs and wants, essential and superfluous.

4.5. Shifting Perspective, Creating Wealth

As consciously pragmatic philosophers, the Stoics did not advocate complete disregard for money. Marcus Aurelius, who was a ruler of the wealthiest empire of his time, stressed judicious usage of resources and conscientious accumulation of wealth.

To truly begin to create wealth, you need to first start with a shift in perspective. You must acknowledge that the creation of wealth is less about earning as much as you can and more about what you do with what you earn. Budgeting, saving, investing, and shrewd use of resources become keystones in this endeavour.

Remember, wealth does not equate to worth. Your value as a person is not tied to your financial status. Therein lies the beauty of stoicism. It allows us to function within the world, amid its chaos and complexity, with a calm, composed demeanor, leveraging tools at our disposal to navigate life's journey.

Our perception of wealth drastically impacts every financial decision we make. Stoicism provides the tools and the mindset to study this perception, understand it, and mould it into a healthier, more sustainable form. By reshaping our mindset and focusing our efforts on what we can control, we open the doors for financial stability infused with stoic serenity.

Chapter 5. The Stoic's Approach to Saving

Drawing inspiration from the enduring wisdom of Stoic philosophers, one must acknowledge that the act of saving, akin to other aspects of personal finance, is highly influenced by our attitudes, beliefs, and wisdom—or lack thereof. A Stoic's approach to saving is based on a profound understanding of human needs along with a keen desire to lead a fulfilled life, deeply grounded in rationality and tranquility.

5.1. The Power of Contentment

According to Stoic philosophy, the root of all dissatisfaction lies in our insatiable desire for more. However, the principle of contentment advises us otherwise. It isn't about constant consumption or accumulating wealth but knowing what we truly need in our lives. Stoicism urges us to question if we genuinely require the materialistic possessions we yearn for or if we should be content with what we possess.

When applied to savings, the power of contentment causes a shift in perspective. Instead of saving with the intention of purchasing, investing or consuming lavishly in the future, a Stoic saves primarily to ensure financial security, thereby eliminating undue financial stress or anxieties.

5.2. The Dichotomy of Control

One of the central tenets of Stoic philosophy is the dichotomy of control, stating that some things are within our control while others are not. Applied to savings, this involves recognizing that despite external economic circumstances, our personal saving habits are completely under our control.

We cannot control market fluctuations, interest rates, inflation, or world events that impact the economy, but we can control our spending habits; how much we save and the financial decisions that compliment our saving efforts. When these actions are guided by wisdom and reason, we claim power over our own financial futures.

5.3. Embracing Minimalism

Stoic philosophy proposes that we should strive to live simply, celebrating minimalism and temperance. It encourages us to eliminate unnecessary spending and be satisfied with the basics that are essential to live.

In savings context, embracing minimalism redirects the resources one might generally spend on unneeded luxuries towards the saving fund. Cutting back on non-essentials and simplifying one's lifestyle stands as a highly effective strategy for implementing a successful savings plan.

5.4. Long-Term Thinking

Stoicism advocates for a long-term perspective towards life, underscoring the importance of patience, perseverance, and delay of gratification. In terms of savings, this translates to persevering with regular saving habits, opting for investments with long-term benefits, and patiently enduring periods of economic downturns or personal financial difficulties.

The Stoics remind us that wealth is transient and not the source of our happiness. Therefore, our savings strategy should be focused on providing long-term stability and financial independence, as opposed to short-term gains.

5.5. Discipline and Consistency

Stoic philosophy calls for strict discipline and consistency in all aspects of life, savings included. It denotes adhering to a wise savings plan and executing it with consistency, despite the challenges that could lead to deviations.

The path to significant savings is not always easy or quick; it demands sacrifice, discipline and an incredible amount of consistency. These tenets of Stoicism applied to savings enables these virtues to flourish, transforming what could be an arduous task into an empowering life decision.

In conclusion, the Stoic's approach to saving is not merely about accumulating wealth. Rather, it is a means of achieving financial security, fostering peace of mind, and creating an opportunity to live a freer, more fulfilled life. It teaches us that by embracing contentment, understanding our control, practicing minimalism, thinking long-term, and applying discipline and consistency, we can tackle the challenge of saving with serenity and wisdom. Our financial future rests in our careful reasoning, rational decisions, and calm persistence—principals rooted deeply in Stoic philosophy.

Chapter 6. Investment through the Prism of Stoicism

The Stoic philosophy, founded in the early 3rd century BC by Zeno of Citium, is a pragmatic methodology valuing logic, personal ethics, and virtue. The stoic perspective refrains from letting fleeting emotions cloud decision-making, emphasizing an analytical, detail-oriented approach - a perfect mindset for the investment world.

Let's explore how applying Stoic principles can enhance your investing technique, steadily leading towards secured financial wellbeing for a fulfilling life.

6.1. Embracing Rational Decision-Making

Stoics treasure rationality, considering it central to proper decision-making. For investments, this means an emphasis on research, due diligence, and critical thinking before venturing into any commitment. Investments must not be driven by anecdotes, speculation, or fear of missing out, but through disciplined, rational analysis and judgement.

In this context, diversification - spreading investments across various areas to minimize risk - resonates well with rational thinking. It reflects technical analysis of market trends, understanding the risk-to-reward ratio, and investment objectives.

It is vital to remember that the Stoic adopts a calm, focused mindset, impervious to the constant turbulence of the financial markets. The ebbs and flows of market dynamics do not provoke impulsive decisions but are observed, analyzed, and slowly reacted to if necessary.

6.2. Valuing Long term Goals and Moderation

Stoics believe that virtues lie in aligning actions with our nature. They advocate self-governance, responsibility, and interdependence, aiming for long-term benefit over short-term gains. This applies to investing, too. Chasing high-yield, volatile options may offer quick profits but invites high risks. A Stoic approach would prioritize stable returns over an extended time, securing gradually built wealth for the future.

Understanding this helps investors maintain a measured, consistent investment approach, insulating against the uncertainties of market economics. Stoic moderation encourages strategic investments, such as low-cost index funds, blue-chip stocks, and other options with historically consistent returns.

6.3. Detachment from Material Possessions

Stoic philosophy advocates detachment from material wealth. Stoics consider wealth to be 'indifferent,' - it is neither inherently bad nor good. Its worth depends on how individuals use it.

While this might initially seem counterintuitive to investing, understanding this detachment brings a fresh perspective. It keeps investors from jeopardizing their financial health by over-investing or making risky moves driven by greed. The Stoic investor seeks financial growth without recklessly attributing happiness or self-worth to monetary success.

6.4. Confronting Negative Outcomes: Premeditatio Malorum

Perhaps one of the most advantageous Stoic practices for investing is the 'Premeditatio malorum' - the premeditation of evils. It involves visualizing possible negative outcomes to prepare mentally and emotionally.

When applied in an investing context, it prepares the investor for all potential outcomes, inducing a sense of preparedness and calm. The Stoic investor cautiously determines their risk tolerance, plans crisis management strategies, and creates safety cushions like emergency funds.

This investment buffering strategy also aligns with Stoic minimalism, urging individuals to live within their means, save, and invest the surplus responsibly.

6.5. The Dichotomy of Control

At the core of Stoic philosophy lies the dichotomy of control – recognizing what is within our control and what is not. This recognition forms an essential part of a Stoic's approach to investing.

Just like the unpredictability of life, the fluctuating market trends are beyond any individual investor's control. Focusing energy on elements within our control, such as our reaction to market changes, our level of investment knowledge, and sticking to our investing strategy, can guide us through market upheavals.

Concludingly, Stoicism's unflinching focus on logic, discipline, and tranquility lends an unruffled approach to investment. The combination of Stoic philosophy and structured investment strategies promotes wise, well-thought-out financial decisions, buffering against unnecessary risks and losses.

By aligning investing with Stoic principles of moderation, detachment, and rational decision making, investors can strive towards financial security with peace and serenity, a testament that when ancient philosophy intertwines with modern finance, the results can be remarkably beneficial.

Chapter 7. Calm in Chaos: Risk Management for Stoics

Understanding the nature of financial risks is crucial to effective management and stability. Much like the proverbial tempest, financial risks can appear seemingly out of nowhere, tossing your plans into disarray. Stoicism, with its focus on tranquillity and control over one's reactions, offers an engaging perspective on how to face these financial storms with calm determination. We will uncover insights from this ancient philosophy, focusing on risk management strategies that align with the core principles of Stoicism.

7.1. The Stoic Philosophy: Pertinence to Financial Risks

Stoicism, a philosophical school established in the 3rd Century BCE, focuses on developing resilience, tranquillity, and virtue through understanding the nature of reality and our place within it. Stoics believed that some things are within our control, such as our thoughts, decisions, and actions, while others are not, like external events or the actions of others. This logic applies handsomely to the realm of financial risks. Risks are inherent in any financial endeavor - but the way we perceive and respond to these risks is entirely within our control.

7.2. Risk and Control: A Stoic Perspective

A fundamental stoic technique is distinguishing between what we can and cannot control. In terms of financial risk, the market forces, economic trends, and global events are all beyond our individual influence. However, we possess full control over our investment decisions, our learning, our level of preparedness, and our reactions. By focusing on these controllable aspects, it's possible to mitigate the impact of financial risks while preserving tranquillity of mind.

Within the domain of control, our first-line defense against financial risk is knowledge. Take time to learn about different forms of investments, understand their returns and associated risks. Choose investment vehicles wisely, keeping in mind your personal financial goals and risk appetite.

Preparation is another key factor under control. Building an emergency fund, diversifying your investments, and keeping insurance are a few ways to protect yourself financially.

7.3. Embrace Uncertainty: A Stoic's Approach

Embracing uncertainty is at the heart of Stoicism. Stoics prepares for the unexpected by expecting it. In financial risk management, this means anticipating fluctuations and planning for losses. This Stoic practice is echoed in the modern financial strategy of always expecting the worst while hoping for the best.

A practical way to embrace uncertainty is by diversifying your portfolio. Diversification entails dividing your investments among different assets - stocks, bonds, real estate, commodities, cryptocurrencies, etc. So your financial health doesn't hinge on one single asset or market. This way, even if one investment vehicle underperforms, others might cover the losses.

7.4. Responding to Financial Losses: A Stoic's Guide

How one reacts to losses can determine their capacity to recover and thrive. A Stoic way to respond to financial losses is by acknowledging the situation, learning from it, and moving forward without anxiety or regret.

Resilience is inherent in a Stoic's nature. With financial losses, instead of ruing over what's lost, focus on what can be learned from the situation. Such insights can help in making wiser decisions in the future, hence enhancing financial resilience.

Living within one's means is a stoic virtue that finds relevance here. Avoiding unnecessary debt and high expenditure lifestyle can provide a buffer against financial shocks and hasten recovery.

7.5. Cultivating Financial Tranquillity: Stoic Techniques

Financial tranquillity, according to Stoicism, comes from an internal state of contentment rather than an external state of wealth. The tranquil Stoic is one who manages risks prudently while remaining detached from the extremes of fear and greed that often accompany financial matters.

One way to cultivate such tranquillity is through negative visualization. By periodically envisaging worst-case scenarios, one can mentally prepare for negative outcomes, reducing anxiety over potential losses.

Lastly, using Stoic journaling to reflect on financial decisions and their outcomes can promote mindfulness and support continuous learning, aiding in effective risk management.

In conclusion, Stoicism provides a fresh viewpoint on financial risk management. It highlights the importance of knowledge, preparation, acceptance, resilience, and tranquillity in navigating financial risks. By employing these Stoic principles, anyone can navigate the chaotic waters of the financial world with coolheaded calmness. The principles posited are sturdy vessels to sail through the storm, preserving peace of mind irrespective of the tempest's ferocity. Remember, the ultimate goal is not just to protect the wallet, but to protect one's tranquil state of mind - for that is the true wealth, according to Stoicism.

Chapter 8. Debt and Desire: Stoic Insights into Consumerism

The allure of consumerism is omnipresent, its impact evident in every corner of society. The central narrative that surrounds us suggests a path to happiness and fulfillment paved with materialistic desires and often leveraged by debt. Before we proceed, let us adopt a stoic's perspective on this understanding of life.

8.1. A Stoic's View on Consumerism and Debt

A stoic thoroughly values freedom, contentment, and rationality, all of which are compromised when we succumb to uncontrolled consumerism and debt. Consumerism, at its core, is driven by desire—an emotion which Stoics view as one of the harmful passions liable to disrupt tranquility and create unnecessary internal turmoil.

Marcus Aurelius, a popular Stoic philosopher, once wrote, "Very little is needed to make a happy life; it is all within yourself, in your way of thinking." It is precisely this mindset that we need to adopt as we strive for financial security by mitigating debt and controlling our desires.

8.2. Identifying and Understanding Desires

Consumerism, fueled by desire, can easily metamorphose into an insatiable beast. It is essential, therefore, to understand and identify our desires. Are they necessary or driven purely by external influence and societal norms? Are we buying things to fulfill genuine needs or to score approval and display status? Stoics urge us to be mindful and aware of our desires, questioning and testing them to distinguish between what's necessary and what's not.

8.3. Economizing Desires: A Strategy

Stoics propose economizing our desires, rather than inflating them. This means curbing unnecessary desires and focusing on needs that contribute to our well-being, rather than our social status. This understanding forms the first step in tackling consumerism from a Stoic perspective.

8.4. 'Negative Visualization': A Stoic Technique to Combat Desire

One can build resilience against the impulses of consumerism with a Stoic technique called 'Negative Visualization.' It encourages us to envision the worst-case scenario if we fail to acquire a desired object. Typically, the worst scenario is far from disastrous, and understanding this can curb our purchasing impulse.

8.5. Debt: The Result of Uncontrolled Desires

Desires left unchecked lead to excessive spending, often culminating in debt. While certain kinds of debt can be beneficial, like a mortgage or an education loan, these should be exceptions rather than the rule.

The cycle of debt and repayment can be an enormous source of stress, reducing our ability to live a peaceful and fulfilled life as encouraged by Stoicism. Rationalizing and measuring our desires against genuine needs can help avert such predicaments.

8.6. Living Within Your Means: A Stoic Principle

Stoicism promotes living within one's means and finding joy in simplicity. It challenges us to reject society's narrative of 'more is better' and to embrace the tranquility that comes from enjoying and appreciating what we already have.

8.7. The Discipline of Debt Repayment

Stoicism emphasizes discipline, commitment, and perseverance—three principles that are particularly applicable to debt repayment. It calls for a sensible approach towards the timely clearing of debts, which includes avoiding new debt and paying off existing obligations as swiftly and efficiently as we can.

8.8. The Peace of Financial Stability

Stoic philosophy advocates that tranquility and joy stem from a balanced mind, not a full bank account. However, achieving financial stability can contribute to a peaceful mind, as it alleviates the stressors stemming from debt and uncontrolled spending.

Understanding and practicing the Stoic insights into consumerism and debt can empower us to sidestep the pitfalls of mindless spending, unnecessary debt, and the unending pursuit of materialistic happiness. This journey towards financial stability is one of self-discovery and mental fortitude. It is a liberating journey, free from the chains of unnecessary desires and debts, and filled with tranquility and contentment. Embrace the wisdom of the Stoics, curb the allure of consumerism, and cultivate a financially empowered and contented life. Step by step, inch by inch, with consistent effort and discipline, we can sail towards a tranquil financial harbor.

Chapter 9. Sustainable Living: The Stoic's Art of Frugality

Among the many intellectual treasures that Stoicism bestows, one stands uniquely applicable to personal finance—frugality, or the art of being economy-wise. Living frugally doesn't mean foregoing all pleasures and becoming a social hermit; instead, it encourages us to question our rampant desires and concentrate our efforts on obtaining that which brings us lasting value. As we tread the Stoic path of frugality, we learn to make conscientious choices that not only lead to substantial financial savings but also promote a sustainable lifestyle attuned to our needs and the wider society.

9.1. The Concept of Frugality in Stoicism

Stoicism, a school of philosophy from Greek antiquity, champions the disciplined use of our resources, both on a personal and societal level. Frugality in Stoicism isn't miserliness; rather, it's the intelligent and considerate application of resources to obtain maximum utility, value, and fulfillment. It demands an understanding of our true needs, demarcated from fleeting wants and illusions bred by societal pressure and consumer culture.

The Stoics remind us that our desires are a bottomless pit, capable of commanding our actions even in the face of detrimental consequences. As such, the practice of frugality in Stoicism involves systematically analyzing and altering our consumption patterns, thereby freeing us from the shackles of incessant desires and paving the way for enjoyable and sustainable living.

9.2. Manifesting Stoic Frugality

Practicing Stoic frugality in our modern world is not a matter of withdrawing from society or completely forgoing its comforts. Rather, it entails weaving frugality into our daily routines, altering our shopping habits, tweaking our home management, and being mindful of our environment. Here's how:

1. Using Items to Their Full Lifespan: One of the cornerstones of frugality is using the things you already own to their longest possible lifespan. Be it clothes, appliances, or cars, when we truly extract the worth of every item instead of pursuing the next big thing, our expenses dramatically decrease.

2. Repurposing: Once an item has reached its lifespan, we shouldn't be too quick to dispose of it. Ancient Stoics like Seneca and Epictetus would remind us to be resourceful, encouraging us to find alternate uses for items before discarding them.

3. Mindful Shopping: Stoicism encourages us to question ourselves before each purchase: Do we need it? Does it provide lasting value? Making it a habit to ask these questions can prevent impulsive buying and save us from the remorse of wasteful spending.

9.3. Stoic Frugality and Sustainability

Stoic frugality extends beyond personal gain and intertwines inextricably with sustainability. By reining in our rampant consumption, we not only bolster our finances but also reduce our carbon footprint, paving the way for a greener and more resilient world.

Stoicism pushes us to value our communal relationships and widen our sphere of concern to include not just ourselves but also the larger ecosystem. As a result, practicing Stoic frugality nurtures an eco-friendly ethos, which harmonizes our personal goals with the health and longevity of our planet.

1. Reducing Waste: Living more frugally often leads to generating less waste. By utilizing all our resources fully, repurposing items, and refraining from impulsive buying, we reduce the waste we produce, which is beneficial both for our environment and our wallets.

2. Supporting Local Economy: Stoic frugality also encourages us to buy locally produced goods, directly supporting the local economy while also reducing the carbon footprint associated with long-distance transport of goods.

9.4. Frugality & Fulfillment: The Stoic Equation

Perhaps the most compelling argument for embracing frugality through the lens of Stoicism comes in the form of a life enriched and fulfilled. We often associate a fulfilling life with material wealth—a notion that Stoicism cordially contests. Stoicism engages us in questioning our assumptions about material wealth and its actual necessity in obtaining happiness.

One might initially think of a frugal life as restrictive and sparse. However, with Stoic wisdom, frugality's true essence unfolds into a conscious lifestyle focusing on intrinsic value over material accumulation. When we practice frugality, we liberate ourselves from the perpetual desire to acquire more, savor the current moment, appreciate what we have, and experience life in its fullest sense.

In essence, Stoic frugality can empower us to lead a truly sustainable life—a life that rests firmly on the spectrum of secure personal finances and promotes well-being, contentment, and sustainability.

Adopting the Stoic art of frugality, we embark on a journey toward financial security seeped in discipline and diligence, discovering along the way the tranquil joy of simplicity and the rich rewards of mindful living along the way.

Chapter 10. Wealth and Happiness: Exploring the Stoic's Perspective

In order to delve into the Stoic's perspective on the relationship between wealth and happiness, we must first understand the fundamental tenets of Stoicism. Stoicism is a practical philosophy which posits that the pathway to happiness, or eudaimonia in the original Greek, is found in accepting the moment as it presents itself, by not being controlled by the desire for pleasure or fear of pain, and by using our minds to understand the world and to do our part in nature's plan.

10.1. The Fallacy of Wealth as the Chief Good

Stoicism contend that wealth is 'indifferent', a preferred indifferent no doubt, but something which in and of itself carries no inherent virtue. Wealth is not the 'Chief Good'. The Stoics assert the only real sustained path to happiness is virtue – moral excellence: the ability to differentiate right from wrong and act accordingly. Wealth cannot buy virtue, nor does one's financial state exempt them from misfortune or guarantee happiness.

The Stoic philosopher Seneca reflected, "It is not the man who has too little, but the man who craves more, that is poor." Stoics suggest that living in want even when we have enough is a state of 'mental poverty.' The pursuit of wealth, if undertaken out of greed, can culminate in an unfulfilled, vacuous existence - a life in servitude to external things that are ultimately transient.

It's of added importance to note that Stoics do not condemn wealth or those who possess it. Rather, they offer a sobering perspective on the dangers of attaching personal worth or subjective well-being to one's net worth. Perhaps this highlights the Stoic discourse: aid others when you have the means, but do not fall into the delusion that wealth equates to character or ensures happiness.

10.2. The Dichotomy of Control

In personal finance, the Stoic concept of the 'dichotomy of control' can be supremely beneficial. This concept is built on the premise that some things are within our control, while others are not. The Stoics suggest we ought to work on the things within our control and accept those that are not.

When applied to finances, it means focusing on how we manage our money, how we save, invest, spend – these are within our control. The state of the economy, the volatility of the financial markets, or unexpected life events that impact our net worth, for instance, are beyond our direct control.

A more practical financial manifestation of this philosophy is building an 'emergency fund'. Paradoxically, by acknowledging that certain things are beyond our control, we prepare ourselves for such events. Building an emergency fund embodies this principle, where we set aside money knowing that life can be unpredictable, and to protect ourselves financially during such situations.

10.3. Align Wealth with Virtue

A core Stoic principle asserts virtue to be the sole good. Virtue, in the Stoic sense, refers to wisdom, courage, justice, and temperance—qualities with inherent worth. They encourage us to perceive wealth, not as an end but as a means that can be utilized for virtuous ends.

This represents a shift from viewing finances solely as a resource for personal interest, to an instrument for benefiting others. To quote Marcus Aurelius, "What isn't good for the hive, isn't good for the bee."

Finance should be wielded as a tool for good—an instrument that can amplify one's capacity to act virtuously. Thus, managing wealth can become a source of satisfaction rather than anxiety when we recognize its potential to contribute to the welfare of others.

10.4. Simplify, Save, Invest

In line with the Stoic principle of living according to nature, we are encouraged to simplify our lives and rid ourselves of excess. This could translate to mindful spending where we focus on needs before wants, avoiding the trap of consumerism where possible.

Applying this principle could also embrace saving and investing. By archiving wealth not for itself, but for providing us with choices and opportunities to act virtuously, we unveil the precision tool that wealth can be – a medium that aids in securing our future, assisting loved ones, and contributing to the welfare of others.

Investing itself echoes the Stoic attitude of perspectivism – perceiving the world as it is, not as we wish it to be. Good investors continually observe, learn, and adjust according to the realities of the financial landscape, parallel to Stoic thinking.

10.5. The Stoic Financial Serenity

A Stoic approach to personal finance guides individuals to embrace financial discipline, make mindful decisions based on wisdom and virtue, commit to lifelong learning, and detach happiness from wealth. It's about moulding a mindset that focuses on things within our control, welcomes simplicity, aligns wealth with virtue and emphasizes the enduring tenet: wealth does not equate to true happiness or worth.

Epictetus, a famous Stoic philosopher, gets the last word: "Wealth consists not in having great possessions, but in having few wants." This underscores the Stoic's perspective on wealth and happiness, steering us toward a financially secure and contented existence.

Chapter 11. Applying Stoic Philosophy: Building Your Financial Future

The journey to a sound financial future often elicits feelings of angst and confusion. However, with the guidance of Stoic philosophy, you can navigate this path with tranquility and discipline. By applying Stoic principles to financial planning, you can cultivate effective strategies not only to safeguard your resources but also to lead a more fulfilled life.

11.1. Principles of Stoicism

A fundamental aspect of Stoic philosophy is understanding what we can control and what we can't. The Stoics preached that most of our emotions like fear, anxiety, and even joy arise from our opinions of events, not the events themselves. We need this wisdom when we deal with financial matters.

Marcus Aurelius famously said, "You have power over your mind, not outside events. Realize this, and you will find strength." Stoicism teaches us to differentiate between what we can control (our values, behaviors, choices) and what lies beyond our control (the economy, stock market performance).

11.2. Embracing Contentment Over Wealth

According to Stoicism, material wealth should not be an end in itself. Instead, one should strive for a prosperous mind and spirit. Money earned and invested can be lost through events beyond our control.

Therefore, placing our joy solely in financial wealth leads to anxiety and stress. Embracing the virtues of self-control, wisdom, justice, and courage can lead to a fulfilled life irrespective of our bank balances.

11.3. Stoic Budgeting: Living within Your Means

Creating a budget is a practical step towards financial stability, yet it aligns perfectly with Stoic teachings. Stoic budgeting entails living frugally, focusing on needs over wants, and robust savings for future uncertainties. By keeping your expenditure in check and saving a significant portion of your income, you not only build a financial cushion but also reduce the fear associated with financial insecurity.

11.4. The Stoic Approach to Debt Management

The stoics encouraged a simple life, free from external influences that could lead to unnecessary desires. Thus, adopting a stoic approach to debt management involves minimizing the use of credit and paying off any existing debts quickly. This not only eliminates financial strain but also offers peace of mind.

11.5. Investing Wisely: Stoic Strategies

Investing should not stir emotions of fear or greed. The Stoic investor maintains a long-term perspective, avoiding frequent changes in investment strategy due to market movements. Patience, discipline, and indifference to short-term fluctuations align with the Stoic idea of focusing on what we can control while disregarding the uncontrollable external factors.

11.6. Saving for a Rainy Day: Building an Emergency Fund

Another key tenet of Stoicism is the acceptance of uncertainty. By saving for a rainy day, you not only acknowledge the unpredictable nature of life but also equip yourself to face any financial obstacles that may arise. A substantial emergency fund serves as a buffer against adverse life events, promoting financial stability and peace.

11.7. Financial Freedom over Wealth Accumulation

In the realm of personal finance, Stoics seek financial independence rather than extreme wealth accumulation. They value the freedom of being financially secure more than the prestige and status of being wealthy. To them, such freedom means being able to maintain a moderate lifestyle without having to worry about financial constraints.

By applying Stoic principles to your financial life, you cultivate resilience, self-control, and acceptance of life's uncertainties. This special report aims to introduce you to the Stoic perspective on personal finance, enabling you to view your financial situation in a new light and effectively manage your resources for long-term financial stability.

www.ingramcontent.com/pod-product-compliance
Lightning Source LLC
Chambersburg PA
CBHW060855260726
48661CB00008B/3285